IMAGES
of England

THE AIRE & CALDER
NAVIGATION

Goole, February 1958. River navigations and docks need regular dredging to remove silt which is continuously deposited. The Aire & Calder had several bucket dredgers for this task, and their introduction in the mid-nineteenth century must have speeded up the process considerably from the former hand-powered 'spoon' dredgers. The winch behind the funnel, together with a similar one forward, was used for moving and positioning the dredger. The funnel could be lowered, the handle visible being for this purpose. The mud raised by the dredger is being loaded into a hopper barge for removal. Gone are the days when you could recognise the boss by his Trilby hat and his having his hands in his pockets! (ABP)

IMAGES
of England

THE AIRE & CALDER
NAVIGATION

Compiled by
Mike Clarke

in association with the
Waterways Museum at Goole

TEMPUS

First published 1999
Reprinted 2000
Copyright © Mike Clarke, 1999

Tempus Publishing Limited
The Mill, Brimscombe Port,
Stroud, Gloucestershire, GL5 2QG

ISBN 0 7524 1715 0

Typesetting and origination by
Tempus Publishing Limited
Printed in Great Britain by
Midway Clark Printing, Wiltshire

British Waterways – 2,000 miles of history

British Waterways runs the country's two-centuries-old working heritage of canals and river navigations. It conserves the historic buildings, structures and landscapes which blend to create the unique environment of the inland waterways, and protects their valuable and varied habitats.

As part of its commitment to the heritage of the waterways, British Waterways was instrumental in setting up The Waterways Trust, which aims to educate the public about the inland waterways and to promote the restoration and preservation of their rich architectural, historical and environmental heritage.

The Waterways Trust is a partnership between British Waterways, The National Waterways Museum at Gloucester, the Boat Museum at Ellesmere Port and the Canal Museum, Stoke Bruerne. The Trust cares for the National Waterways Collection, the country's pre-eminent collection of canal artefacts, documents and boats which are on view to the public at all the museums.

The Waterways Trust also manages the British Waterways Archive, a unique collection of inland waterway records dating back to the late seventeenth century and containing the largest documentary and photographic resource of its kind in Britain. Supported by the Heritage Lottery Fund, the archive is the subject of an ambitious project to make the collection available to all via the Internet. The new Cyber Archive will, for the first time, create a single catalogue of Britain's canal archives, revolutionizing research into the history of the inland waterways.

For more information about British Waterways call 01923 20 11 20 or visit the website at www.britishwaterways.co.uk.

For access to the archive, or to get up-to-date information about the Cyber Archive project, call 01452 318041.

Contents

The River Aire above Leeds Bridge c.1865. A pier of the bridge can be seen on the left-hand edge of the picture. This was the old three-arched stone bridge (replaced in 1873 by the present bridge) on which cloth was sold around the time of the formation of the Aire & Calder Navigation in 1699. It formed the limit of the navigation's rights, the river upstream of the bridge being controlled by the Leeds & Liverpool Canal Company following its formation in 1770. The boats are typical of those which used the navigation from its earliest days, being around 60ft long by14ft wide and capable of carrying 40-50 tons of cargo. Boards have been fitted around the hold of the nearest boat so that the maximum tonnage could be loaded. (LCL)

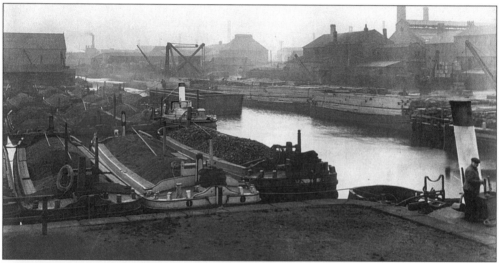

Leeds New Dock around 1900. A variety of cargoes were handled here: timber, chemicals and general cargoes. Off the picture to the right is the Potato Wharf, there being a considerable traffic in vegetables from Lincolnshire. In the centre can be seen three or four 'Tom-Puddings', the container boats used mainly for the coal export trade. They were used occasionally for other goods when boats were unavailable, and these may have brought iron ore from Goole. The importance of the navigation to Leeds' coal supply can be judged by the large group of boats awaiting unloading at wharfs on the river. The two tugs formed part of a large fleet which, at this time, operated day and night on the navigation, towing dumb and sailing boats between Goole, Leeds and Wakefield. To pass under some bridges their funnels had to fold down – the rest for the funnel is clearly visible on the tug in the foreground.

Introduction

The first proposal to make the rivers Aire and Calder navigable was put forward in the 1620s. Britain's textile industry was suffering from a trade depression and a textile merchant from East Anglia suggested making several rivers navigable, both to improve the facilities for the trade and as a job creation scheme for unemployed textile workers. Nothing happened, but by the 1690s the textile trade in West Yorkshire was expanding rapidly and improvements to transport were needed.

For centuries, York had been the centre for this industry in Yorkshire and cloth was carried there by road from the growing West Yorkshire district. The involvement of York annoyed West Yorkshire merchants, as they wanted to control the sale and distribution of their own products. Merchants from Leeds and Wakefield came together to push forward a scheme to make the rivers Aire and Calder navigable from the Ouse to their towns.

The proposed navigation received its Act of Parliament in 1699, and was fully open from Airmyn, just above the mouth of the Aire, to Wakefield and Leeds by 1704, though boats had been using the rivers prior to this. Leeds Bridge was the head of navigation on the Aire, and for years the local cloth market had been held on the bridge. At the time Daniel Defoe visited the town in the 1720s, the market had moved to Briggate, but he does describe the town as having an 'abundance of wealthy merchants in it.' It was a small group of these merchants, together with others from Wakefield, who paid for the construction of the navigation. After a decade or so of financial problems, it developed into a huge success, making vast amounts of money for its owners. Having seen the achievement of these Yorkshiremen, merchants all over Britain were soon promoting their own river navigations and canals. The success the Aire & Calder was a major factor in shaping the Industrial Revolution.

Although the navigation made its owners wealthy, little profit was reinvested in the navigation until the Leeds & Liverpool Canal was proposed in the late 1760s. Because the navigation was then in a very poor state, there was a proposal to bypass it with a canal to Selby from the Leeds & Liverpool Canal's terminus in Leeds. This galvanized the navigation's owners into action, and they employed John Smeaton, a Leeds man who is regarded as the world's first professional civil engineer, to design and make improvements. In order to allow boats to carry greater loads, he suggested both deepening the locks and lengthening the lock cuts to avoid shoals. One of the shallowest sections was on the tideway to Airmyn: several plans for avoiding this were considered before the scheme of Smeaton's assistant, William Jessop, for a canal to Selby was finally adopted.

Improvements were continued in the last decades of the eighteenth century, particularly to control water usage. There were several water mills on the Aire whose owners and millers were constantly lowering water levels to make it difficult for fully-loaded boats to use the navigation. Over the years, the navigation purchased these so that there was less interruption to trade on the waterway. Lock cuts were also lengthened on the Aire above Castleford, bypassing shallows and ensuring that sufficient depth of water was available, particularly in the summer. The owners of the navigation were also involved with the promotion of the Barnsley Canal, one of the 'Canal Mania' projects of the early 1790s. As with many waterways built at this time, it was never particularly successful, but it did allow coal from the Barnsley coalfield to reach the Aire & Calder, thereby increasing profits on the navigation.

By the early 1800s, coastal sailing ships were increasing in size and were having difficulty reaching Selby up the twisting course of the Ouse. In order to overcome this problem and further improve the navigation, the Knottingley and Goole Canal opened in 1826, allowing much larger vessels to use the navigation. At its eastern end, the Aire & Calder built the new canal port of Goole which still thrives today. The shallow and winding Calder, from Castleford to Wakefield, was also bypassed by a new canal over the following decade. By this time profits from the navigation were enormous, with shareholders receiving dividends of 150% – one and a half times their original investment being paid back to them each year!

In 1825, Thomas Bartholomew commenced work as engineer for the navigation. His workshops and home were at Lake Lock, on the river below Wakefield, and it was here that his son, William, was born. Between them, they were to completely modernize the navigation. Locks were lengthened and deepened, steam towage introduced, and William, after the death of his father, designed the compartment boat or 'Tom Pudding' system. This was highly profitable, carrying millions of tons of Yorkshire coal to Goole for both British and continental markets. He was also responsible for the construction of the New Junction Canal which links the Sheffield & South Yorkshire Navigation to the Aire & Calder.

The company was nationalized in 1948, becoming part of British Waterways in 1973. They were responsible for enlarging the locks up to Leeds to 700-ton standard in the 1960s and 1970s. New cargo-handling facilities, such as the Knostrop Depot at Leeds, were built, and only recently two miles of new canalized river and a lock have been opened at St Aidans to allow opencast mining to be extended over the old course of the river.

The Aire & Calder Navigation is not typical of Britain's inland waterways. It has been improved and enlarged throughout its three hundred year existence, allowing it to continue to provide water transport at a competitive rate. Several British canals and river navigations managed to compete successfully with railways in the late nineteenth and early twentieth century, but only the Aire & Calder continues to carry large tonnages of cargo today.

Although the navigation still carries well over a million tons of goods annually, leisure use has been growing in recent years. Better facilities, landscaping and improved water quality has attracted pleasure boating, towpath walking and even fishing. At the same time, waterside tourist attractions like museums, wild-life reserves, restaurants and pubs are enabling the general public to appreciate the Aire & Calder's heritage and wildlife, and the waterway is seen as a key element in a campaign to extend West Yorkshire's tourist appeal.

One
A Historical Review

A view of Leeds taken from Thoresby's *Ducatus Leodensis*, a history of Leeds, published in 1715. On the left is the uppermost lock on the recently opened navigation. It is typical of navigations at the time, the lock cut merely allowing boats to bypass the weir. There was only one long cut or canal section on the navigation in its early days; the Crier Cut was built about 1709 above Woodlesford to avoid Greywood Lock and a shallow section of the river. The locks were also typical of the time, with a wooden floor and foundation on which were built masonry walls. They were about 60ft long by 14ft 6in wide. Boats could be loaded up to 3ft in depth when the river was full, but much less at low-water periods in the summer.

The first page of the Act of Parliament, passed in 1699, which allowed the construction of the navigation. The Aire was to be improved upwards from Weeland, the river below remaining in its natural state. Shallow water and sandbanks on this stretch were to become a problem and canals, first to Selby and then to Goole, had to be built to bypass it. Unlike with previous navigations, most of the undertakers were merchants rather than aristocratic land-owners. From this time, those involved with trade and industry were to become more and more influential. The passing of the Aire & Calder Act marks an important step in the developments which were to result in the Industrial Revolution.

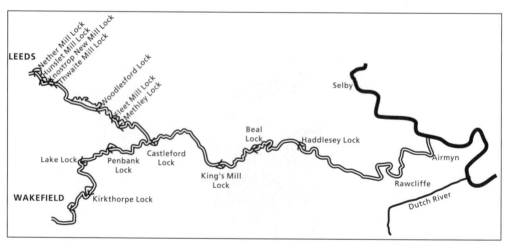

A map of the navigation as it was from around 1715. Crier Cut, above Woodlesford, had been built by this time. It did away with the need for Greywood Lock, but resulted in Woodlesford Lock being deepened, a factor which caused subsequent maintenance problems. The Aire was tidal as far as Knottingley, and boats had previously sailed this far up the river regularly to transship cargoes here. There were also several boat-yards, the town continuing to be a boat-building centre until recently. When the locks and weirs were built below Knottingley they caused the river to become silted. This is always a problem on navigable rivers, but the tidal nature of this section created much greater problems and resulted in proposals, carried out in the 1770s, to avoid the lower reaches of the river.

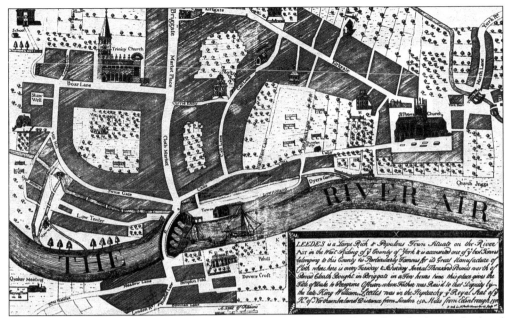

A map of Leeds from 1725 showing boats waiting just below Leeds Bridge which was the head of navigation until the Leeds & Liverpool Canal opened to Leeds in 1777. The boats are sloop rigged and not the square-sailed keel rig with which Yorkshire's waterways are often associated. There is a warehouse on the northern bank of the river, convenient for the Cloth Market in Briggate. Simpson Fold, to the south of the river, was where the navigation built its imposing offices at the start of the twentieth century.

The earliest boats using the navigation could only carry around thirty tons. They developed into the keel which could carry around 100 tons. This one is probably on the Ouse. The cock boat behind was used for getting ashore when anchored, taking lines ashore for moving the boat around docks, and other similar purposes. (WMG)

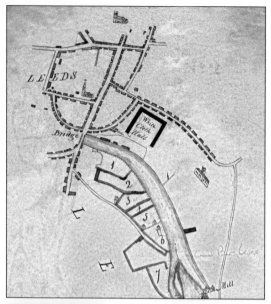

By 1770 trade in Leeds had increased dramatically as a result of the navigation. Amongst the most important developments was the construction of the Coloured Cloth Hall and the White Cloth Hall where merchants could trade unhindered by the weather. The cloth market moved away from Briggate, but the White Cloth Market did not move that far and it was still convenient for the navigation's wharves close to Leeds Bridge.

A horse-drawn Leeds & Liverpool Canal boat, the *Mary of Bingley*, being shafted down river at Leeds, c.1920. Following the Leeds & Liverpool Canal obtaining its Act in 1770, there was considerable agitation for a Leeds & Selby Canal which would avoid the need for using the Aire & Calder as this was in a poor condition. Little of the profits had been reinvested, but the proposed canal forced the undertakers of the Aire & Calder to start improving their navigation and to build the Selby Canal. The *Mary* was owned by John Barron & Son who were coal merchants in Bingley. It is a typical coal boat from the Yorkshire end of the Leeds & Liverpool Canal, with wooden chimneys for the cabin stoves, and no coamings to the hold. As there is no towpath on this stretch of the river, boats had to be shafted or wait for a tug. Most of the other boats are Aire & Calder flyboats which were towed by steam tugs, though there is one sailing keel which almost certainly belonged to a private owner. This too would have used the tug service when travelling on the navigation. (LCL)

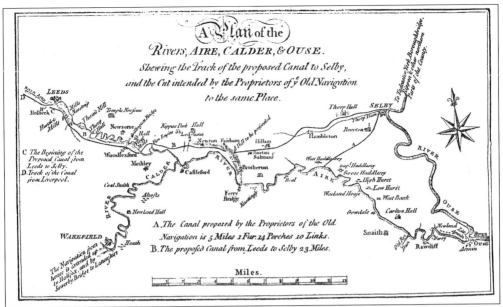

The Selby Canal was designed by William Jessop to counter the proposed Leeds & Selby Canal, illustrated here, and was set out to avoid the shoals found on the lower reaches of the Aire. Jessop was John Smeaton's assistant for several years, learning how to organise and design engineering works under him. Smeaton originally suggested a canal to the south of the river as part of his improvement scheme for the whole navigation in 1770. Jessop then suggested one to the north of the river, with the canal to Selby finally decided upon to counter the proposed Leeds & Selby Canal. Selby was at this time an important port on the Ouse, with boats trading both around the coast to London and across the North Sea to the Continent. The canal was opened on 29 April 1778.

Bridges over rivers were expensive, particularly when the river was wide. Before the navigation, fords could be used, but afterwards a depth of water sufficient for boats had to be maintained. Ferries were introduced to overcome the problem. This is the one at Airmyn, on the tidal section of the Aire, being used by local hauliers to cross the river in 1907. (WMG)

13

Castleford weir and the mill now operated by Allinson's. The original lock at Castleford was on the left bank of the river, just out of sight on the left of the photo. Over the years, the mills on the navigation were purchased by the Aire & Calder, thereby ensuring sufficient water for boats. Several mills, besides this one, are still operable. Water transport used to be an important feature of their use, grain being delivered through the overhanging canopy. The two rearmost keels are of clinker construction – with overlapping planking – putting the date of the photo at around 1900 at the latest. (WMDC)

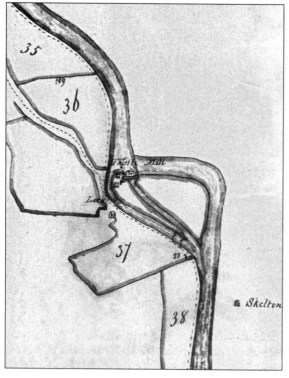

Thwaite Lock and Mill in 1772, showing how the navigation used existing mill weirs by building short sections of canal with a lock at one end to bypass the mill. This area has changed completely. Above the mill a new section of river has been built and the old line filled up. The present lock is also further up the river, with a view downstream appearing on page 96 showing the removal of the old lock island located somewhere near field 35 on this map.

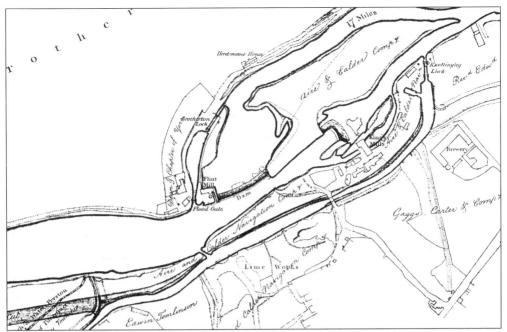

The mills and locks at Knottingley, c.1820. Until the navigation purchased these mills in the 1770s, they were a continual source of problems. The miller often ran down the level of water above the weir causing boats to become grounded. Before the river was improved in the 1770s, depth was always a problem for boatmen. In dry weather, 'flashes' of water were created by lowering the boards on a weir, boats floating over shallows below on this flush of water. However, such profligate use of water was a problem for the miller who needed as much water as possible for his water wheels. The conflict of interest was reduced after the navigation purchased the mills on the river, though they had to pay dearly for them.

Too much water, in the guise of floods, was another problem on river navigations. Here two dumb boats – possible Aire & Calder Navigation flyboats – have been washed over Kirkthorpe Weir and have finished up at Stanley Ferry. This section of river was bypassed for navigation c.1830 and the wooden structure on the right protects the aqueduct which carries the new canal across the old navigation.

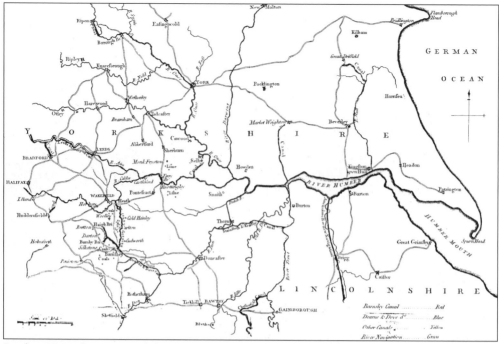

By the 1790s, the output of the coalfield in the Calder Valley could not satisfy demand, so the Barnsley Canal was built to tap the rich seams of coal around the town. The canal was never very successful due to problems with water supply, but it provided a useful source of coal traffic for the Aire & Calder. The navigation leased the canal from 1855 and then purchased it in 1871.

Heath Locks, with a horse-marine and his horse towing a boat up the locks. The horse-marine operated independently of the boat, providing his service for a fee. They often worked regularly with particular boatmen. On the Aire & Calder, tugs were usually used to tow boats, but on smaller canals, with many locks, horse power provided a more economical solution. (WMG)

A Leeds & Liverpool Canal boat enters the Calder from the Barnsley Canal, loaded with coal for the towns on the banks of the Leeds & Liverpool. It was an important market for Barnsley coal and one of the last regular traffics to use the canal. (WMG)

The Barnsley Canal's main cargo was coal, and it was subsidence caused by coal mining that led to its closure shortly after the Second World War. There was a major breach at Littleworth, near the junction with the Dearne & Dove Canal, in 1946, following which closure was recommended. The canal was abandoned in 1953. (WMG)

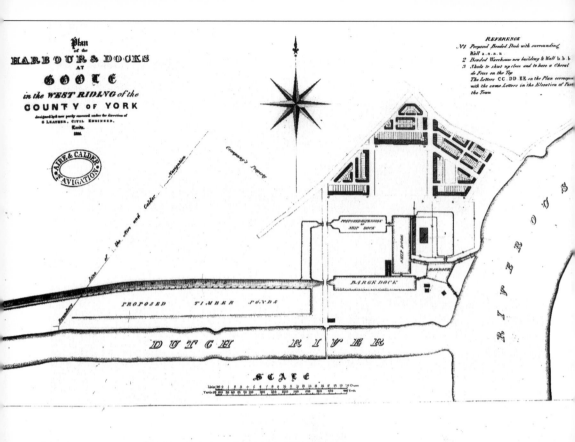

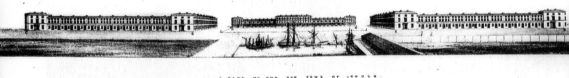

By the start of the nineteenth century, the port of Selby was proving inadequate for modern shipping and the Selby Canal was too shallow and hindered the navigation's trade. Moreover, because boats were increasing in size, it was thought beneficial to increase the size of the locks. The plan eventually settled upon to overcome these problems was for a canal from Knottingley to Goole. At that time, Goole was nothing more than a collection of cottages at the entrance to the Dutch River, the entrance to the River Don constructed by Vermuyden to improve land drainage in the seventeenth century. Here docks and a spacious new town were to be laid out, though the latter was never completed to its original plan as suggested at the bottom of this map. (ABP)

A view of Goole from a balloon around 1880 showing how quickly the town and docks developed. Aldam, Victoria and Railway Docks had been added to the original system, and the town was now reaching out beyond the Hull to Doncaster railway (NER) which opened in 1869. The Lancashire & Yorkshire Railway had served the port since 1848. (ABP)

A compartment boat train makes its way towards the cutting at Knottingley, the only major work, apart from building Goole itself, on the whole line of the new canal from Knottingley to Goole.

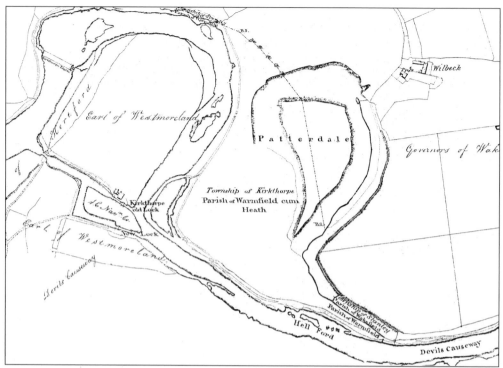

With the opening of the Knottingley & Goole Canal, the Calder from Castleford to Wakefield also needed improvement. The river was shallow and winding, conditions suggested by 'Hell Ford' and 'Devil's Causeway' on this 1820s map of the locks at Kirkthorpe. The new lock here was built in 1815, allowing vessels 18ft in width to reach Wakefield. However, none so large could use the navigation until the Knottingley & Goole Canal opened, as the locks at Haddlesey and Selby had not been enlarged!

Two keels on the river above Castleford weir, c.1920. Although the locks up to Wakefield had been enlarged, the keel remained the main cargo carrier until the mid-nineteenth century. Steam towage then became common, allowing larger boats to navigate the waterway. (WMDC)

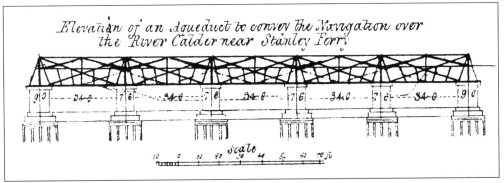

Stanley Ferry Aqueduct was the major work on the new section of canal. The original design of 1825 shown here, was by George Leather and was for a cast iron trough probably supported by wrought iron ties. Six piers were needed, three of which were to be erected on the river bed. The construction of these could have interrupted the flow of traffic on the river and this may have been the reason why the design was changed. Instead, Leather designed a trough, supported by wrought iron ties, which was hung from a cast iron arch. He built two bridges to a similar design over the navigation – at Crown Point in Leeds and for a tramway at Astley – both using cast iron arches with suspended roadways.

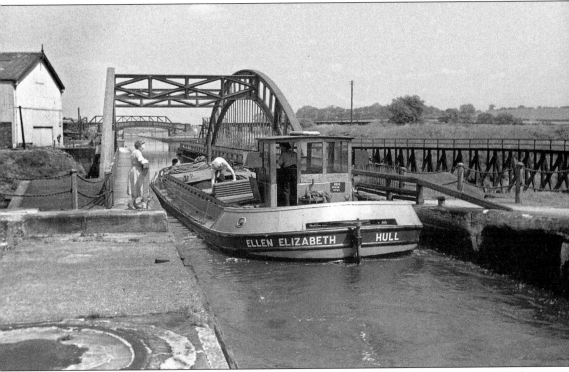

Stanley Ferry Aqueduct was opened on 8 August 1839. It was built by canal contractor Hugh MacIntosh, the ironwork coming from William Graham & Co's Milton Ironworks at Elsecar. The aqueduct became the limiting factor for boats on this section of the waterway. It has been bypassed by a new concrete structure which allows for a greater waterway cross-section and thus larger vessels. The building on the left was Stanley Ferry maintenance yard's compartment boat repair shed. (BW)

The Aire upwards from Castleford had been deepened to seven feet and the locks widened to eighteen feet by April 1835. In 1829 Leeds was a busy centre, where a large warehouse had been erected on the north side of the river close to Leeds Bridge. Sailing vessels reaching Leeds must have had masts which could be lowered, but they would have to be raised so that cargo could be transshipped to and from their holds. Cranes were available lower down the river for removing masts to make the passage up the river easier, but many boats still kept their masts aboard. The boatmen probably thought that the bit of extra work involved in working around the mast justified saving the money paid for craning out the mast.

In the mid-eighteenth century, steam towage was introduced on the navigation. Tugs towed perhaps four boats at a time and the locks were lengthened so that all the vessels and the tug could pass through in one 'penning'. (BW)

The other reason for lengthening the locks was the introduction of 'Tom Puddings' in 1863. Originally, the compartments were pushed in trains of up to twelve. The compartments were joined together by chains running the full length of the 'tow', the composite 'boat' being bent to go around corners by steam cylinders pulling on the chains. A cylinder can be seen here alongside the funnel. This system had been replaced by around 1900, the compartments being towed, as here, without any means of steering them. (WMG)

The Leeds engineering firm of Fowlers, well-known for their traction engines and ploughing engines, constructed an experimental chain towage system, where boats were hauled along a chain laid on the canal or river bed. This method was used successfully for many years in France and Germany, but never got beyond the experimental stage on the Aire & Calder. Instead, Bartholomew, the navigation's engineer, designed improved propellers for steam boats.

Right from the construction of the Knottingley & Goole Canal, there had been plans for a link to the River Don Navigation which would provide a route for coal and other traffic between Goole and the valley upwards to Sheffield. A scheme was finally agreed in 1890 between the Aire & Calder and the Sheffield & South Yorkshire navigations, and the canal opened in 1905. There was a bridge provided over the junction with the Aire & Calder Navigation to allow horses towing boats between Goole and Castleford to continue on their way without hinderance.

There was one lock on the canal, at Sykehouse, 215ft long by 22ft wide, capable of handling a full train of compartment boats. There were also several swing bridges on the canal, each provided with a bridge house similar to the lock house at Sykehouse, seen here shortly after the canal opened.

There were two aqueducts on the canal where it crossed the rivers Went and Don. The Went joined the Dutch River about a mile downstream, and this from where the boat must have come, the Dutch River being navigable from Goole to Stainforth where there was a lock into the Stainforth & Keadby Canal. The foundations for the aqueduct have been piled to protect them not just from high tides, as this part of the river is tidal, but also from flooding resulting from heavy rains upstream. On rare occasions, the river has overflowed the aqueduct.

By the time the New Junction Canal was built, the navvy had become more a general labourer. Lifting equipment, such as the steam crane in the distance, had taken away much of the hard work, though the life of the itinerant labourer must still have been arduous under the eyes of the bowler-hatted foreman.

Bulholme Lock during enlargement in the 1960s. The old curved lock bottom had to be cut away to make the sides vertical so that new 700-ton standard vessels could use the waterway. (WMDC)

At St Aidans, just upstream of Castleford, a large open-cast coalmine was opened close to the navigation. Too close, in fact, as the bank between the two gave way. For four days the Aire ran upstream from Castleford until the opencast site was completely flooded. As a result, the lines of the river and navigation have been moved westward and a new lock constructed. This aerial view was taken on the day of the lock's official opening. (HA)

Two

People

The Aire & Calder had men and boats working on many of the waterways in the north-east of England, though all were involved with traffic connected to the navigation. Some boats worked through Fall Ings Lock at Wakefield onto the Calder & Hebble Navigation, such as this Aire & Calder Navigation flyboat at Thornes Lock on the Calder & Hebble. It is probably returning from the ACN depot at Dewsbury. Note the safety rope around the gunwhales, suggesting that the boat also worked down the tideway to Hull. (WMG)

Perhaps the most important engineer to work on the navigation was William Hamond Bartholomew. The son of Thomas Hamond Bartholomew, the navigation's engineer from 1825 to 1853, he became engineer at the age of twenty-two, and continued in the post until 1895. Even then he remained a consultant until his death in 1919. Not only did he oversee the complete rebuilding of the navigation, with all the locks being lengthened under his control, but he developed improved methods of steam towage, in particular the compartment boat system. It was one of the most cost-effective coal transport systems invented. With a secure position as engineer to the country's most modern waterway, and working alongside William Aldam, the navigation's dynamic chairman, there was no need for Bartholomew to advertise his expertise. Consequently little is published about his work, but he certain ranks as one of Britain's foremost waterway engineers. (WMG)

Bartholomew was born here, at the Lake Lock maintenance yard a few miles downstream of Wakefield. He must have taken in much of his engineering expertise as a child, growing up amongst the workshops looked after by his father. Saw mills and blacksmiths' shops provided most of the materials necessary for maintaining the waterway, and iron boats were also built here. The workshops were eventually moved to Stanley Ferry, access to these workshops becoming more difficult after the new line of canal to Wakefield had been built in the 1830s.

Message by Telephone. Time 27/3/ 1895

From *Bartholomew* | To *Grayburn*

There will be no loading charges payable to A.C.N. on manure if delivered on Botter grange wharf a charge of 5/- must be made for canal tolls no dock dues being charged

Huntington now Bennett

Bartholomew was also responsible for the day-to-day management of the waterway from 1876. As this telephone message shows, he authorized freight rates and wharfage charges. The Aire & Calder had its own telephone system, with origins in 1861 when a telegraph company was allowed to erect telegraph poles along the towpath in return for free usage by the navigation. Subsequently a telephone system was installed which remained in operation until the 1970s.

William Bartholomew was buried in his family's grave at the church close to Lake Lock. In fact the grave almost overlooks the site and it is easy to imagine him still keeping an eye on developments on the navigation. His father's gravestone is the one laid flat on the ground.

In 1816, Joseph Priestley was appointed Head Clerk to the navigation. His father had held a similar post on the Leeds & Liverpool Canal, working assiduously for that canal from 1770 to 1817. His son worked just as hard for the Aire & Calder, finally retiring in 1851. He is best remembered for his guide to *Navigable Rivers and Canals*, published in 1831. Even today, it provides a useful source of information for waterway historians.

Priestley was based at Wakefield in this office. From here, he controlled the day-to-day operation of the navigation. Following Priestley's retirement, Leeds became the headquarters of the navigation, particularly after the construction of the Dock Street offices.

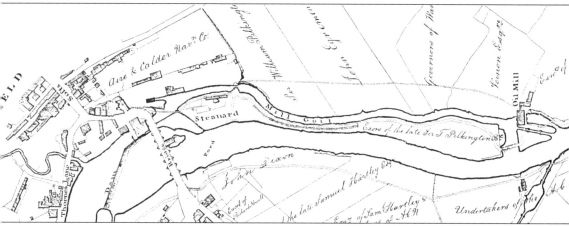

The original terminus of the navigation in Wakefield was the mill race, with the feed coming from above Wakefield Bridge. The entrance lock was alongside the Oil Mill powered by the mill race. The term Steanard is used to describe land between a mill race and a river. Joseph Priestley's office is one of the Aire & Calder buildings directly opposite the northern end of the bridge. The terminus declined in importance after the Calder & Hebble Navigation's Fall Ing Lock was built. An extension to this lock cut, seen here on the extreme right, was built jointly by the two navigations and opened in 1812. It gave the Aire & Calder access to new warehouses on the river above the weir.

The navigation usually employed engineers with a high reputation. The original plan was set out by John Hadley, who was an established engineer. John Smeaton was responsible for the improvements of the 1770s. A local man from Austhorpe, a village on the outskirts of Leeds overlooking the Aire, he is regarded as the first professional engineer. His assistant, William Jessop, was particularly involved with the Selby Canal which was his first independent job, and he went on to engineer several important British canals. Thomas Telford provided advice on the improvements in the first half of the nineteenth century, though the actual work was often superintended by George Leather, pictured here. He was a local engineer from Bradford who went on to establish an important practice in Leeds. (WMG)

Before the river was made navigable, there were several fords crossing it. These were converted into ferries and the navigation had to provide ferrymen to convey people and animals across the river for a small charge. Some of these continued in use until recently. Here is an early twentieth century picture of the one operated by Stan Pollington at Hunslet.

Aire and Calder Navigation.

NOTICE.

To Inspectors & Superintendents of the Aire & Calder Navigation; also to Captains of Dredgers and Fly Boats, and others.

DROWNED PERSONS
(DISCOVERY and INTERMENT) ACT, 1886.

The above Act provides that any person finding a Dead Human Body in the Navigation, shall within Six Hours give notice of the finding of such dead human Body to a Police Constable, who will make the necessary arrangements for its removal and interment, and the Superintendent of the Police for the District in which such dead human body shall be found and brought to bank, will pay the person first giving such information the sum of **FIVE SHILLINGS.** Any person finding a Dead Human Body in the Navigation, and not giving notice as aforesaid, will be liable to a Penalty of **FIVE POUNDS.**

Aire and Calder Navigation Office,
Leeds, November, 1886.

W. H. BARTHOLOMEW.

SAMUEL MOXON, PRINTER, QUEEN'S COURT, BRIGGATE, LEEDS.

One of the less savoury jobs which employees had to undertake is suggested here. The notice was issued in 1886 at a time before medical attention was freely available, and those with severe illness would sometimes use a waterway to end their suffering. However, the five shillings paid for the discovery of a body must have made a useful addition to the income of those working on the waterway.

Leeds Lock around the start of the twentieth century. The two men are wearing 'gansies', thick jumpers knitted with traditional patterns often worn by boatmen. At one time, lock-keepers were not paid by the company, but relied upon the penny given to them by every boat passing through the lock, a tradition which continued until recently, even after lock-keepers were paid a wage. Leeds Lock has an unusual layout. The original lock is on the right of the lock-keepers office, with the newer, wider, lock on the left dating from the early nineteenth century. The gates in the foreground were added later that century to allow a number of vessels to pen through the lock together. This became important after the introduction of steam tugs as it reduced drastically the time taken for several boats to pass through a lock. The cast iron paddle gear is typical of that found on the Aire & Calder Navigation. The weir maintaining the level of the river in Leeds is behind the timber piled up on the island between it and the lock, an indication of how much traffic was being carried on the navigation at this time. Space for storage was always at a premium. Access to the New Dock, now known as Clarence Dock, was under a bridge used by the road on the left. (BW)

Water transport relies heavily on cargo handling, the boat crew often having to help in this respect. Here, at the new Knostrop Depot in the late 1960s, a cargo is being transshipped from a British Waterways barge to one of their lorries. On the right an oil tanker makes its way up to one of the two oil terminals alongside the river in Leeds. One can be seen just through the flood lock in the distance.

At Goole, large gangs of stevedores were employed until quite recently. Here timber is being transshipped into railway wagons at West Dock in 1960. Today timber is bundled and handled by machinery and the operation needs fewer men. (WMG)

AIRE AND CALDER NAVIGATION.

CARRYING DEPARTMENT.

Schedule referred to in attached Agreement.

AMOUNTS PAYABLE TO THE CREWS OF FLY BOATS, PER ROUND TRIP.

ROUND TRIP (There and Back).	BARGES.		LONG BOATS.		OTHER FLY BOATS.	
	MASTER.	MATE.	MASTER.	MATE.	MASTER.	MATE.
BETWEEN	s. d.	s. d.	s. d.	s. d.	s. d.	s. d.
Goole and Hull	6 11	4 6	5 10	3 10	4 4	3 5
Goole and Leeds or Wakefield	13 7	10 1	10 3	7 6	9 3	7 2
Leeds and Bradford or Shipley ...	....	....	....	....	3 0	2 2
Leeds and Barnsley	....	....	....	...	11 7	7 9
Leeds and Rodley, Kirkstall, or Watson's Wharf, Leeds .... }	....	....	...	....	2 0	1 8
Goole and Barnsley	....	....	....	....	11 2	8 2
Wakefield and Mirfield, Calder Wharf, Dewsbury, or Barnsley .... }	...	....	...	....	2 0	1 8
Wakefield and Brighouse, West Mills, Cooper Bridge, or Elland ... }	....	....	....	....	3 0	2 2
Wakefield and Huddersfield, Whitacre Bridge, Sowerby Bridge, or Halifax.... }	....	....	....	....	3 11	3 4
Goole and Castleford	..	....	....	....	7 9	5 3
Goole and Whitley	....	....	....	....	6 3	4 6

(Left margin: THROUGH BOATS.)

TURN-BACK BOATS AND EXTRA ROUND TRIPS.						
Wakefield and Mirfield	...	....	...	....	6 3	5 3
,, and places West of Mirfield	....	....	...	....	9 3	7 11
Leeds and Bradford or Shipley	....	....	...	....	9 3	7 11
,, and Kirkstall or Watson's Wharf, Leeds	....	....	...	....	3 1	2 8
,, and Knottingley	....	....	...	....	6 3	5 3
,, and Castleford or Rodley	....	....	...	....	6 3	5 3
Brighouse or Elland and Huddersfield	....	....	, ...	....	3 1	2 8
Halifax and Sowerby Bridge	....	....	...	....	3 1	2 8
Shipley and Bradford	....	....	...	....	3 1	2 8
Dewsbury and Calder Wharf	....	....	....	....	3 1	2 8

Allowance for taking on extra Cargo at Wakefield :—

For Brighouse, Cooper Bridge, West Mills, Whitacre Bridge, and Elland .... }	Not less than 5 and up to 10 tons	2 0	1 6
	10 tons and up to 25 tons *3d. per ton additional.		
For Huddersfield, Halifax, and Sowerby Bridge .... }	Not less than 5 and up to 10 tons	2 11	2 0
	10 tons and up to 25 tons *3½d. per ton additional.		
For Calder Wharf, Dewsbury, Barnsley .... }	Not less than 5 and up to 10 tons	1 10	1 2
	10 tons and up to 25 tons *2d. per ton additional.		

(Above 25 tons to be paid for as extra trip).

Allowance for taking on extra Cargo at Leeds :—

For Bradford—Not less than 5 and up to 10 tons	2 0	1 6
10 tons and up to 25 tons *3d. per ton additional.			
For Rodley, Kirkstall, or Watson's Wharf, Leeds }	Not less than 5 and up to 10 tons	1 10	1
	10 tons and up to 25 tons *2d. per ton additional.		

(Above 25 tons to be paid for as extra trip).

* *This tonnage payment to be apportioned three-fifths to Captain and two-fifths to Mate.*

NOTE.—Where a Single Trip is made and not a round Trip, a proportionate amount is payable.

The Aire & Calder operated two distinct transport departments: the carrying department handled general cargo while the coal department operated the compartment boat system. Although kept separate for accounting purposes, boatmen were moved between them. Conditions and pay were agreed with the unions and the rates published. This schedule dates from c.1910.

Until the recent introduction of wheel-houses, conditions for boatmen were exposed. Here J.W. Calvert steers one of the steam-powered compartment boat tugs. Note the boiler casing in the foreground with its safety valve cover and whistle. Escaping steam must have been an added hazard for the steerer. WMG)

A typical keel-man waits for the water levels to equalize before opening a lock gate. Note the gansey he is wearing which, together with corduroy trousers, was the standard wear of many boatmen on the wide canals in the north of England.

Three
Down the Navigation

The River Aire below Leeds Bridge, with a sloop waiting to unload on the right. The brick warehouse behind is the Flyboat Warehouse, built in the 1820s for the general cargo trade. Although the term 'flyboat' conjures up images of boats working non-stop, on the wide northern waterways it meant general cargo boats, often working to a timetable. (LCL)

An early photograph – possibly taken in the 1860s – showing the end of the old stone-built Leeds Bridge and three clinker-built boats: the planking is overlapped and the edges are rivetted together. This was the old Yorkshire method of construction which originated in Scandinavia. The last boats of this type were built towards the end of the nineteenth century, construction subsequently being of carvel type where the planks butt up against each other and the joint is caulked with oakum. (LCL)

Leeds, probably around 1890 as most of the wooden keels are of clinker construction. The number of boats loading and unloading gives some idea of the importance of the navigation to Leeds. (WMG)

The stern of an iron keel, the *Semloh of Goole*, at Leeds, possibly in the 1960s. Note the three tillers: one standard, one short for use in locks and one bent upwards to make steering easier when loaded with a bulky cargo. (LCL)

A view of the river below Leeds Bridge, with a variety of flyboats and tugs. The flyboat on the right is loaded with a fairly light cargo. This protrudes out of the hold and is covered with hatch covers and then sheeted over. (LCL)

The first steam coaster to reach Leeds, *Progress of Goole*, against the wharf opposite the Flyboat Warehouse in 1900. Note the Mission Hall, one of several on the navigation. It seems in pristine condition, so perhaps the crowd have assembled for its opening. There was a second mission in Leeds, next to the canal basin at the end of the Leeds & Liverpool Canal. Both missions were supported by their relevant canal authority.

Leeds Lock with the Co-op tug *President* passing through in the early 1970s. This was the last regular traffic on the navigation to use towed dumb boats, coal being carried from waterside collieries to the Co-op's coal wharves in Leeds. (WMG)

All types of coal were carried on the navigation. This Leeds wharf, photographed in 1955, was one of several used for household coal. (WMG)

A view of the river at Crown Point Bridge, c.1920. (WMG)

Knostrop Fall Locks, with the railway line crossing the river by a swing bridge. At the time of the railway's construction, in the 1880s, a ship canal to Leeds along the line of the navigation was being considered, and the railway company was forced to build a swing bridge. It was built in the open position and then swung across the canal – the only time it ever moved!

Knostrop Fall Locks from the railway bridge, with three Leeds & Liverpool-sized boats passing downwards, probably *en route* to the coalfield. The first boat is steam-powered and towed the two dumb boats behind. The original line of the river is off the picture to the left, with the new line, built early in the twentieth century, on the right. (WMG)

An aerial view of traffic on the river at Stourton, *c.*1960.

Skelton Grange Power Station in the early 1970s. It was served by Cawoods using barges capable of carrying about 200 tons. Here one of them is half unloaded. (WMG)

Coal was a major cargo, with a variety of types for a variety of uses, from house fires to power stations. In the 1970s at Savile Basin, above Castleford, several different types of boat, including Cawoods *Ann*, are being loaded. (WMG)

The coal staithe at Astley in 1977, with one of Cawoods boats loading for Skelton Grange Power Station. The loading basin was originally the main canal, and a lock at the end carried boats down into the Aire. When the navigation was enlarged in the middle of the nineteenth century, the canal was extended to a new lock. The boat from which the picture is taken is heading towards that lock.

James W. Cook & Co. Ltd's motor tanker *Kittiwake C* heads out of Castleford Flood Lock and up the Aire towards Leeds towing the dumb tanker *Auk C* behind. The Calder can be seen on the left. (BW)

A horse-drawn Aire & Calder Navigation Flyboat on the Calder, just below Wakefield. The bridge crosses the bottom of Fall Ings Lock, leading to the Calder & Hebble. The original Aire & Calder Navigation terminus was reached via a lock just out of the picture on the right. (WMG)

A view from the bridge looking down on Fall Ings Lock, with loaded compartment boats ready to pass through the lock before being assembled into a train and then towed down to Goole. (WMG)

Fall Ings Lock, with a maintenance boat heading back to Wakefield Depot. Judging from the audience, school must just have finished. Although part of the Calder & Hebble Navigation, this lock and the short length of canal were built by the Aire & Calder.

Lofthouse Basin at Stanley Ferry, c.1970. Originally, coal was loaded here from a railway feeding the staithe on the right. However, by the time this photo was taken, this had ceased and the vessels may well be engaged in carrying grain which was unloaded here then. (WMG)

Hargreaves yard at Castleford in the 1970s with a push-tow unit loaded with coal heading down to Ferrybridge Power Station. This system was a development of the compartment boats, several of which await loading in the background. The large brick building on the right was formerly used by the Aire & Calder for 'weighing' boats to find out their draft for a given weight.

The waterway at Castleford has changed several times over the years. The first lock was by the weir, then moving to near Hargreaves drydock, just off the picture at the top of the page. With Tug No.3 moored at the entrance, this is the third lock and it seems to be still in use even though Bulholme Lock, seen in the distance, has been opened. The remains of the third lock can still be found on the river bank, though the lock cottages have disappeared. (WMDC)

After boats had been weighed at Castleford, two brass plates were made, marked with the tonnage for a particular draft, and fixed to the boat's stem and stern post. When they were loaded, the weight they were carrying could be measured and the correct toll charged. This Tally Card would be filled in and sent to the traffic office so that the boat owner could be invoiced. The *Alice of Shipley* was a Leeds & Liverpool horse boat, purchased from Joseph Clarkson by Abraham Kendall, a Shipley coal merchant, in 1896. It was broken up in 1914. Coal boats would carry any bulk cargo such as the copper ore loaded here for Bradford. Jonathan Rendell worked for the Leeds & Liverpool at the Leeds warehouse where he must have dealt with tolls, thus passing on the Aire & Calder's invoice to Abraham Kendall. With partners, he took over two coal carrying businesses based in Shipley in 1922, eventually taking over the business. He retired in 1953.

Aire and Calder Navigation.
TALLY CARD.

August + Date 13· 1896
Ex Dog Duck Wharf
13 - 1895

alice of shipley Capt
Benton Mr Kendellacaunt
fore Plate 52 Tons
after Plate 48 Tons of copperoar
for Bradford

Name of Tallyer, Joseph Rhodes

The oil traffic continues today, though this photo of Cook's *Kittiwake C* passing through Bulholme Lock with a variety of other traffic dates from the 1960s. Note the odd shape of the lock, brought about by repeated enlargements. (BW)

Fryston Colliery basin in the early 1970s. Just off the river between Castleford and Knottingley, this was one of two such basins on this section of the river, the other being at Wheldale Colliery. (WMG)

The tanker *Beldale* just after leaving the cutting at Knottingley, heading towards Castleford and Leeds in 1973. (WMG)

An old postcard showing the canal and industry at Knottingley. Glass works, a pottery and limestone quarries were all served by the waterway.

Lyric delivering sand to Knottingley Glassworks in 1970. (WMG)

Historically, Knottingley is an important boat-building centre. Before the Knottingley & Goole Canal opened in 1826, boats were built on the river bank. Subsequently, boatyards were set up around the junction at Bank Dole. Here a compartment boat train, drawn by diesel tug *Hatfield*, passes Harkers yard in the 1970s. Bank Dole Lock and the Selby Canal were reached by the arm which left the main canal on the right. (BW)

Haddlesey Lock, which used to allow boats to pass onto the tidal section of the Aire, is now derelict. In this 1970s photograph, however, it is still readily recognizable. (WMG)

There was a basin at Selby for use by canal craft, but sea-going and coastal vessels had to lie in the tidal river. The opening of Goole, with its docks, led to the rapid decline in Selby's importance as a port, though it continues to be used by coasters today. Here, pleasure boats and commercial barges are tied up above the lock in the 1960s.

The flour mill at Selby was slightly upstream from the entrance to the canal. In the mid-1970s it was still a bustling part of the port with both coastal shipping and barges serving its wharves, seen here from *Leeds Magnetic* as it makes its way downstream.

The flour mills at Whitley Bridge in 1973. Grain was always an important traffic on the navigation as the population of industrial West Yorkshire grew. (BW)

Unloading the *Freda Careless* at Whitley Bridge in 1973. Although the majority of the cargo could be handled fairly easily by the elevator, labourers had to ensure that the last few tons were unloaded. (WMG)

The motorised keel *Goldilocks* makes its way up the navigation near Rawcliffe in the 1960s. (BW)

The mill at Rawcliffe with a motorised keel being unloaded, *c.*1970. The cargo has been bagged so it may be destined for storage before forwarding by road. (WMG)

Tug No.2 passing the railway sidings alongside the canal just before Goole. The loco shed at Goole was close to the navigation and may have taken water from the navigation as happened at some other Lancashire & Yorkshire Railway sheds close to canals. (WMG)

An empty motor barge passes Timms Mill, through South Dock Bridge and into Barge Dock, one of the two earliest docks at Goole. Barge Dock has been widened considerably over the years, while South Dock, beyond the bridge, was opened in 1912. There were several boat-builders around Barge Dock, Webster & Bickerton occupying a yard on the right of the picture where there used to be a slipway.

Four
Goole and the Tideway

Barge Dock c.1890, with Aire & Calder Navigation flyboats waiting to be towed up the navigation. At this time the road bridge, from where the photograph was taken, had just been converted into a swing bridge, though a smaller fixed bridge for barges was not built until about 1909. It was constructed on the right of the picture. (WMG)

An aerial view of the northern half of the docks taken in the 1920s. In the foreground is Ouse Lock, built in 1838, wide enough to suit the paddle steamers of the time. Victoria Lock, beyond, opened in 1888. It is longer and narrower to suit the propeller-driven ships of that time. From the locks, ships entered Ouse Dock and then passed through Lowther Bridge into Ship Dock, one of the two original docks – together with Aldam Dock – dating from 1881, visible on the right. Beyond are Railway Dock (1848), Stanhope Dock (1891) and West Dock (1912) in the distance. The curved street corners of the older part of the town were characteristic of Goole. Three boat hoists, Nos 2, 3 and 5, can be seen, as well as the railway coal hoists in Railway Dock. The original entrance locks are off the picture to the right, as is Barge and South Docks and the Knottingley & Goole Canal. (WMG)

AIRE AND CALDER NAVIGATION.

GOOLE DOCKS

NOTICE IS HEREBY GIVEN

THAT

ALL TRAFFIC OVER THE LOWTHER BRIDGE

WILL BE

STOPPED

from One o'clock on Saturday Afternoon, the 6th November, 1915, for about three days to enable adjustment of the Bridge to be carried out.

Engineer's Office,
Leeds, 29th October, 1915.

BY ORDER.

JOWETT & SOWRY, Printers & Lithographers, Albion Street, Leeds.

A 1915 notice from the Engineer's Office announcing the temporary closure to road traffic of Lowther Bridge.

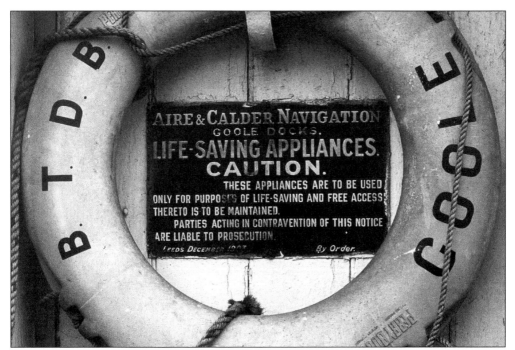

AIRE & CALDER NAVIGATION
GOOLE DOCKS.
LIFE-SAVING APPLIANCES.
CAUTION.
THESE APPLIANCES ARE TO BE USED
ONLY FOR PURPOSES OF LIFE-SAVING AND FREE ACCESS
THERETO IS TO BE MAINTAINED.
PARTIES ACTING IN CONTRAVENTION OF THIS NOTICE
ARE LIABLE TO PROSECUTION.
LEEDS DECEMBER 1907.   By Order.

Goole Docks were opened by the Aire & Calder Navigation in 1828. On nationalization, in 1948, they passed to the Docks & Inland Waterways Executive, then becoming part of British Transport Docks Board – hence the initials on this lifebelt. Today they are owned by Associated British Ports and are handling more traffic than ever.

The *Equity* was built in 1888 for the CWS and passed to the Goole Steam Shipping Company in 1906. After an eventful career, including being seized in Hamburg at the start of the First World War, she was broken up in 1931. She is seen here passing through the bascule bridge between Ouse and Railway Docks which was replaced around the First World War time and is now known as Lowther Bridge. (WMG)

Ouse Dock, with Nos 1 and 2 Boat Hoists, seen from the corner of Ship Dock. Note the sliding bridge in the centre of the photo. (WMG)

Railway Dock shortly after it had been extended in 1891. The tower on the left is a railway coal hoist, provided for emptying coal from railway wagons into ships. (WMG)

A postcard of Aldam Dock around 1900 showing both the variety of vessels and the variety of cargoes handled by the port at this time. At the time there was no containerization. (WMG)

Although a great variety of cargoes were handled, none came anywhere near the tonnage of coal transshipped. Not only were some eight coal hoist of different types provided, but several cranes, such as the hydraulic fifty-ton crane in Stanhope Dock seen here, were also used, amongst other duties, for coal transshipment. (WMG)

The docks have been extended and improved regularly. Here Railway Dock is being enlarged by the addition of the basin on its western side just before the First World War. The railway in the background fed one of the two railway coal hoists, the bridge carrying the line over Bridge Street. (WMG)

New electrically-driven hydraulic pumps were installed by Hodgart & Barclay in the 1930s. Here they are under construction in their Paisley works. (WMG)

Shipping continued to increase in size during the early part of the twentieth century, so a new entrance lock was planned to accommodate this. Called Ocean Lock, it was under construction when this photo was taken in 1937. Note the shipyard on the banks of the Ouse downstream of the Dutch River. (WMG)

Ocean Lock, shortly after opening in 1938. (WMG)

Two views of the transit shed built in the 1920s alongside Aldam Dock. Until quite recently, cargoes were often handled in the open air and almost always by manual labour. Men would assemble early in the morning and were taken on as required for that day's work. Those living in Old Goole, on the other side of the Dutch River were sometimes delayed by the swing bridges being opened and thereby lost the opportunity for a day's work. Times were set when the bridges would not be opened, but circumstances sometimes caused them to remain open for too long.

Railway workers and their horses take a pause from work near Aldam Dock in 1928. (WMG)

Docks on the former Lancashire & Yorkshire Railway system were always a Mecca for ancient shunting locos, and Goole was no exception as this view of West Dock – c.1950 – shows. At this time, the *Alt* was operated by Associated Humber Lines, being built in 1911 and scrapped in 1954. (WMG)

Railways have been important for the development of Goole, despite the port's owners being the Aire & Calder Navigation. The Ghent & Antwerp Shed, seen here in 1921, was between Aldam and Ouse Docks. Note the containers. (WMG)

Although the docks handled a wide variety of cargoes, coal was predominant. Here a sailing ship is loading coal at a railway hoist in Railway Dock. (WMG)

A container service was introduced by British Railways on their Copenhagen service in the 1950s. Designed to fit on a standard railway wagon, they were very much the forerunner of today's containers. A similar system was used on the navigation using smaller fibreglass containers.

A Bennett Line advert showing locomotives being shipped onto one of their ships by the fifty-ton crane in Stanhope Dock. (WMG)

The SS *Mopsa* of the Bennett Line, known for the red cross on the funnel of their vessels. The Bennett Line operated between Goole and Boulogn and the *Mopsa* was sunk on this service on 16 July 1916. (WMG)

The *Irwell* was built for the Goole Steam Shipping Company's Rotterdam service in 1906. In the 1930s the firm became Associated Humber Lines as part of an amalgamation and the *Irwell* was scrapped in 1954, not long after this photograph was taken. (WMG)

The River Ouse up to Goole could be difficult to navigate. Not only were there several sharp bends, but as it was tidal, vessels had to rely upon arriving at the correct time to ensure there was sufficient depth. The jetty at Blacktoft was provided for boats waiting for a tide giving enough depth for them to reach Goole or wharves further up the river.

AIRE AND CALDER NAVIGATION.

OUSE (LOWER) IMPROVEMENT ACT, 1884.

BLACKTOFT JETTY.

NOTICE IS HEREBY GIVEN that

NO MORE THAN NINE VESSELS

will be allowed to moor to this Jetty

at any one time except with the written

consent of the Harbour Master or Jetty

Master.

BY ORDER.

LEEDS, *December, 1907.*
594—1907

SS *Aire* of the Goole Steamship Company on the Ouse, *c.*1928. She was built in 1886 and broken up at Hook, just around the corner from Goole, in 1930. (WMG)

The Aire & Calder had its own wharf on the River Hull at Wincolmlee. This 1954 photo shows gravel being unloaded with the Thames spritsail barge *Will Everard* moored to the opposite bank.

Barges also used the docks, loading and unloading cargoes direct to ship. Here *Kappa* and *Delta* of British Waterways are transshipping cargo in Hull Docks. (BW)

Five

Tom Puddings

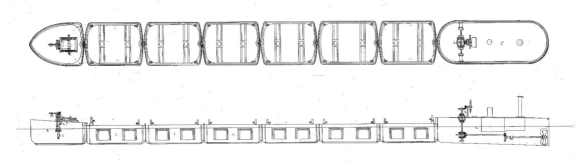

In order to compete successfully with railways, an innovative system was required. William Bartholomew provided this in 1863 with compartment boats, often called 'Tom Puddings'. Each compartment carried around 40tons of coal. Hydraulically operated hoists were erected at Goole which lifted the compartments out of the water and then turned them over, emptying their cargo into the hold of a waiting ship. This is the patent drawing for the compartments, showing the original method of pushing them and using steam-operated chains for bending the train of boats so they would go round a corner. Subsequently it was found more practical to tow the compartments in trains, usually comprising twenty-one compartments. Perhaps the system can best be described as 'The Railway on the Water'. Between 1863 and 1912, five hoists were built to cope with the increasing trade, tonnages reaching a peak of over one and a half million tons just before the First World War. The system continued to be used until 1985, but recently Goole has suffered the ignominy of importing coal.

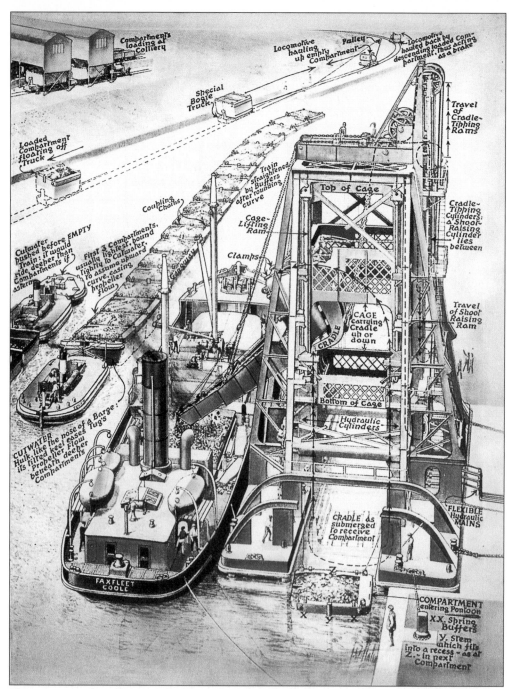

The system explained pictorially in an illustration published in *The Graphic* in the 1920s. The hoist illustrated is No.4, the only floating hoist. It was designed to be moved about the dock system, but difficulties in providing the hydraulic power supply limited its use. Originally, it was berthed on the south side of South Dock, being moved to the north side in 1926 when No.5 Hoist was moved from West Dock and re-erected in South Dock. (WMG)

Unlike the subsequent steel-framed hoists, the first hoist in Ouse Dock was built with a wooden frame. All the equipment for the hoists was supplied by Armstrong Whitworth, the Newcastle firm who were closely associated with the development of hydraulic machinery. (BW)

A view of No.2 Hoist in Ouse Dock with the *Sanfry* laying alongside for loading. All types of coal were handled, the benefit of the system being that it reduced breakage. Note the compartment in the foreground which has coamings. At one time compartments were considered for carrying general cargo which would need protection from the weather. Bartholomew's original design was for a sectional boat, rather than a system confined to coal carrying. (WMG)

No.4 Hoist is manoeuvred through South Dock Bridge on the way back to her mooring on 21 May 1957. The move was required so that the mooring could be dredged.

Nos 4 & 5 Hoists in South Docks, c.1960. The wooden tower on the right houses the accumulator, a vertical weighted cylinder which acted as a reservoir for high pressure water used to operate the hoists. (BW)

The bottom of No.2 Hoist, with loaded compartments awaiting unloading. One compartment in the cradle is being tipped and an empty compartment has already been unloaded. (WMG)

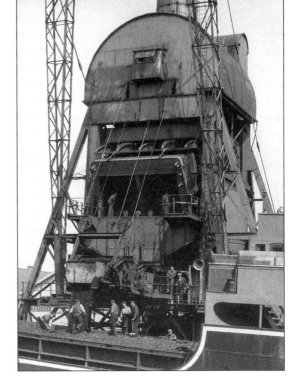

No.3 Hoist with a compartment in the process of being tipped. The hoist was operated from the cabin in the roof: two men looked after the compartment, ensuring that it was clamped in the cradle and emptied correctly, with a further group of men on the boat who trimmed the cargo. (WMG)

When shipping coal, it is always important to keep down the amount of breakage. This is usually done by controlling the rate at which the coal falls which was the object of this anti-breakage device fitted to No.5 Hoist. The chute and hopper were filled from a compartment in the conventional way, the coal being discharged into the ships hold by a short conveyor, the whole device being turned to ensure that the ship's hold was completely filled. (WMG)

Loading at No.3 Hoist with trimmers leveling off the coal to ensure that the ship floats evenly and making the cargo less likely to shift. The conveyor was part of an anti-breakage system. (WMG)

Both compartment and general traffic tugs awaiting their next job lie outside the Goole workshops in South Dock, c.1930. Nos4 and 5 Hoists can be seen, with South Dock Bridge in the distance. (WMG)

From Goole, the empty compartments were towed up the navigation to the coalfield. The Jebus, or bowpiece, was pushed in front of the tug, here No.14, and the compartments towed close-up behind. (WMG)

The compartments were particularly susceptible to the wind when empty, the train often curving away downwind. Other boats on the navigation had to ensure that they passed on the upwind side.

The compartments were loaded from a number of staithes ranging from the most basic, to more refined ones such as the one in this drawing of Fryston Colliery Staithe.

In order to reduce breakage, compartments were drawn out of the water on a bogie and taken by rail to St Johns Colliery, near Stanley Ferry. After loading they made the return journey and were then lowered back into the water. An average of around 1,000tons per week were handled in this way, perhaps four compartments per day. (BW)

After the compartments had been loaded, they were made up into trains for towing to Goole. Here a train begins its journey down the navigation from near Park Hill. Because the compartments were loaded and thus deep in the water, the jebus was fitted to the head of the train to help divert the flow of water from the tugs propeller. (WMG)

In the twentieth century a train would normally comprise around twenty-one compartments, over twice the number originally proposed when the compartments were to be pushed. However, this number could be exceeded, and here thirty-eight compartments are under tow. It was probably the difficulty of splitting the train when passing through locks which limited the number which were normally formed into a train. (BW)

Steam tug No.4 with a loaded train in tow passes the Lofthouse Colliery basin, just above Stanley Ferry aqueduct, in the early 1960s. The loading staithes were fed by the colliery's railway and the tips are typical of the simple coal-handling facilities usually provided. Both compartments and conventional barges were handled here. Today the basin is a marina, but several of the original features can still be seen. (BW)

In the 1950s and 1960s the steam tugs were replaced by diesel powered ones. Here *West Riding*, one of the new diesel tugs, tows a train of compartments towards Goole on the New Junction Canal in the 1970s. (WMG)

Assembling a train after loading at Doncaster on the Sheffield & South Yorkshire Navigation, prior to heading for the New Junction Canal and Goole. (WMG)

The original design for the compartments envisaged their use for carrying other cargoes. A few did carry grain to mills above Wakefield, and coke, pitch and iron ore were also carried. This 1960s photo shows some loaded with wire, either because there were insufficient general cargo boats or to act as warehousing. (WMG)

Six

Boat-building and Repairs

One of several new barges built for the Docks & Inland Waterway Executive shortly after nationalization. This may be the *Gamma*, one of the motor boats named after Greek letters, before its launch on 21 April 1949. The dumb boats they towed were just given numbers.

Compartment tug No.12 or 13 is under construction at Webster & Bickerton's yard, at Goole, on 13 December 1904. The yard was on Barge Dock, just next to what was called the Canal Swing Bridge and is now known as South Dock Bridge. (BW)

RIVER DON
(DUTCH RIVER)
GOOLE

A postcard of Old Goole showing the shipyards at the time when they were still around Barge Dock. Following completion of the enlargement of the dock after the First World War, shipbuilding was moved across the Dutch River almost to where this photo was taken from. (WMG)

Goole Shipbuilding & Repairing Company built many ships, particularly after moving to the yard at the entrance to the Dutch River, in Old Goole.

Bluebird, Malcolm Campbell's yacht, under construction at Goole Shipbuilding in the 1930s. It was probably the best-known vessel to have been built at Goole. (WMG)

The *Sidney Billbrough*, seen here on 28 December 1950, did not need to go far for delivery. She worked from Yorkshire Tar Distillers works opposite the shipyard, just behind the building on the right.

Harkers also built sea-going boats, such as this one pictured just after launching. I wonder if anyone ever stood on the towpath to get a better view during launches such as this! Large boats would have to be ballasted down for delivery so that they could get under the overbridges between Knottingley and Goole.

Compartment Tug No.13 outside the Aire & Calder's workshops at Goole. The overhanging workshop on the left contains an overhead crane for lifting out compartments for repair. (BW)

Compartments under repair in the navigation's Goole workshops. Standard parts were kept in stock so that such repairs could be undertaken quickly and economically. (BW)

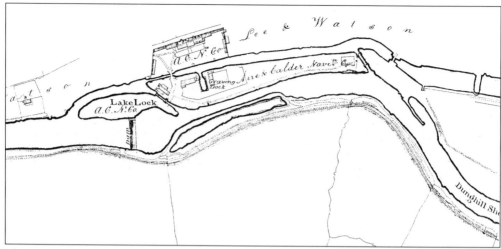

The navigation's first workshop was at Lake Lock, on the river between Castleford and Wakefield. This plan, from around 1820, shows the workshop site, opposite the graving dock. The buildings remain, but almost everything else has disappeared because the river has been improved to reduce the chance of flooding. The lock and weir on the left were built during the initial phase of construction three hundred years ago. The lock on the right dates from later improvements around 1800, the same time as Lee and Watson took the navigation to court over their canal to Bottom Boat, off the map to the right. The dam built across this canal by the Aire & Calder can just be seen on the right.

Stanley Ferry workshops replaced those at Lake Lock, the long wooden building on the right being used for compartment boat repair. Today it is where many of British Waterways' lock gates are made. The basin on the left is where coal was loaded from St Johns Colliery, while the motor boat, *Olive Pittwood*, towing a dumb boat, has just passed through the aqueduct on her way from Wakefield to Goole. (BW)

Icebreaking was sometimes needed to keep the navigation open in winter, as shown in this 1963 photo where one of the compartment boat tugs, *Whitwood*, is seen employed on this task. In the 1950s the tugs were named after collieries rather than just having numbers. (WMG)

Steam ships serving Goole needed to be serviced and supplied. Coal for ships bunkers was quite an important traffic on the navigation, and here a coaling gang take a break from their arduous task. Coal was shovelled into large wicker baskets on board a barge and then lifted onto the ship using the vessel's steam derricks. (WMG)

Compartment boats, because of their low freeboard, were always prone to sinking. Hand-powered lifting screws were generally used to raise them sufficiently so that they could be pumped out. (BW)

The lifting screws were also used during lock repairs, particularly for the larger gates used at Goole. This 1959 picture shows new gates being installed at Victoria Lock. (ABP)

Some idea of the size of the lock gates on Victoria Lock can be gauged here during the fitting of new middle gates in 1957. Stone masons are dressing the quoin, the rounded rebate against which the gate turns. (ABP)

Silt is always a problem for both canals and river navigations. Here workmen are removing the mud from the floor of Victoria Lock in 1956, prior to the gates being repaired. (ABP)

Divers often have to be used, particularly on deeper navigations such as the Aire & Calder. They are needed to clear away rubbish from the sills against which the gates seal, as well as for rubbish drawn into the ground paddles. This diver is working at Leed Lock, probably clearing the sill. Boat No.5 in the background is probably one of the Co-op's coal barges.

Dredging was undertaken continually to ensure the correct depth of water. The Selby Canal was a particular problem, with silt entering from the rivers at both ends of the canal. Here a dredger is working on the canal in the 1930s. (WMG)

AIRE AND CALDER NAVIGATION.

LIST OF CANAL CONSTABLES.

No.	NAME.	RANK.	ADDRESS.
1	Barnham, Richard	Inspector	Leeds.
2	Whitaker, Arthur	Labourer	Ramsden's Bridge.
3	Mitchell, James	Captain of Dredger No. 2	Castleford.
4	Gamble, Ralph	Labourer	Fleet Mills.
5	Scott, Edward	Foreman Joiner	Castleford.
6	Hartley, Henry	Labourer	Ditto.
7	Dickinson, James	Ditto	Oulton.
8	Dinsdale, James	Foreman Stone Mason	Swillington Bridge.
9	Morton, William	Labourer	Woodlesford.
10	Whiteley, George	Foreman Carpenter	Lake Lock Yard.
11	Armitage, Charles E.	Inspector of Boats	Castleford.
12	Towning, Matthew	Watchman	Leeds Yard.
13	Connell, John	Lock-keeper	Selby.
14	Calvert, Tom	Wharfinger	Goole.
15	Rutter, Edward	Coal Hoist Foreman	Do.
16	Pickard, Richard	Inspector	Do.
17	Earnshaw, Thomas	Berthing Master	Do.
18	Baker, William	Ditto	Do.
19	Lovell, Thomas	Foreman	Fly-Boat Warehouse, Goole.
20	Gale, Henry	Ditto	Bond ditto, ditto.
21	Bradley, Henry	Ditto	Ouse Lock, Goole.
22	Young, Thomas	Ditto	Goole.
23	Bateman, John G.	Ditto	Do.
24	Burden, William	Lock-keeper	Birkwood.
25	Lovell, William	Labourer	Fly-Boat Warehouse, Goole.
26	Brown, John	Coal Tug Foreman	Goole Docks.
27	Ingleby, Christopher	Assistant Harbour Master	Ship Lock, Goole.
28	Matterson, John R.	Lock-keeper	Lemonroyd Lock.
29	Pollard, George	Ditto	Whitley Lock.
30	Croft, John	Ditto	Ditto.
31	Peaker, George	Ditto	Ferry Bridge.
32	Campfield, Peter	Ditto	Ditto.
33	Goward, Robert	Labourer	Hunslet.
34	Law, John	Ditto	Castleford.
35	Robinson, John	Ditto	Brotherton Lock.
36	Jolliffe, Martin	Lock-keeper	Woodnook.
37	Teal, George	Ditto	Bulholme Lock.
38	Brook, John	Ditto	Pollington Lock.
39	Baxter, James W.	Foreman Carpenter	Stanley Ferry.
40	Boothroyd, John	Foreman	Lake Lock Yard.
41	Rhodes, John	Lock-keeper	Altofts Lock.
42	Boothroyd, William	Engine-man on Dredger No 2	Lake Lock Yard.
43	Smith, Joseph	Foreman	Royston Bridge.
44	Abson, Thomas C.	Lock-keeper	Heath Lock.
45	Taylor, Joseph	Labourer	Walton.
46	Smith, Thomas	Lock-keeper	Do.
47	Harker, George	Labourer	Knostrop Cut Turn Bridge.
48	Redshaw, William	Ditto	Bullough Bridge
49	Abson, John	Foreman	Knottingley.
50	Chapman, John	Labourer	Rothwell Haigh.

330—1902

From the 1840s, canals were allowed to have their own constables, and the Aire & Calder certainly had several, armed with pistols. By the time of this notice they had become more akin to today's special constables, though they did receive a retainer and expenses for such items as oil for their hand lamps.

The *Hartel* in Ocean Lock after being raised following grounding and sinking in the Ouse in 1951. The shallow, winding waters of the Lower Ouse have always needed careful navigation. (WMG)

This barge, sunk in the entrance to Barge Lock, required part of the dock system to be drained before it could be raised. (WMG)

Ferrybridge Lock during reconstruction and enlargement in the 1960s. Note the curve to the bottom of the walls to the side of the lock. In order to increase the size of boats, masons had to remove these and make the lock walls vertical. The footbridge behind is the old portcullis one, which had to be raised for boats to pass. This has been replaced with a permanent raised overbridge.

Stanley Ferry aqueduct was the main restriction to increasing boat size on the Wakefield arm. In 1981 a new aqueduct was built, the trough being cast from concrete and then slid into place. Here it has reached half way on its journey across the river. (HA)

Further pictures of the 1960s reconstruction and enlargement of the waterway to 700-ton standard. Above Thwaite Island is being removed to allow larger vessels to enter Thwaite Lock. Below, the navigation is being widened by piling, using a steam pile-driver, the boiler for which is on the boat. Subsequently, the old bank was removed by dredging.

Seven

Traffic

Clarence Dock, Leeds, in the 1960s, with a variety of smaller craft. Leeds Lock, on the other side of the road in the background, limits the size of boats which can reach this part of the navigation. (BW)

A new warehousing facility, complete with garages for delivery lorries, was built at Knostrop in the 1960s. This is the model of the site that was used for publicity. (BW)

Although it was built to accommodate vessels up to 700-ton standard, general cargo boats of this size were never built and traffic continued being carried in smaller vessels.

Modern handling equipment was provided in an attempt to fit in with the growth of road transport. It came too late as the container was just about to change the whole face of transport. Apart from a few specific traffics, water transport can only really compete with road transport on long-haul routes where its relative cheapness of carriage can counter the expense of lifting cargoes into and out of a boat. Water transport is more environmentally friendly than other forms of transport, but at the moment the cost of environmental damage is still regarded as of less importance than direct costs.

John Hunt & Sons had been general carriers on the navigation for many years, and continued to use the warehousing at Dock Street in Leeds until about 1975. By then it was becoming uneconomic for them to continue and the warehouses stood idle for a number of years.

Kappa, one of the British Waterways barges named after Greek letters, unloading at Dock Street, Leeds, in the 1960s. These were the same warehouses used by John Hunt & Sons, and today they have been converted into flats and houses. (WMG)

The smaller 'Sheffield-sized' barges continued to use the navigation until the end of general cargo carrying. Above, *Waterbird* passes under the portcullis bridge over Ferrybridge Lock in the early 1960s, while on the right an empty boat *Rye* makes its way into Goole Docks for another load in the late 1970s. It will probably be loading a cargo for Rotherham, reached via the New Junction Canal and the Sheffield & South Yorkshire Navigation.

Kittiwake C, one of Cory's oil tankers, makes its way through Castleford past Hargreaves yard in the 1960s towing the dumb boat *Auk* C. In the background the other boats which have penned through Bulholme Lock at the same time follow the two oil tankers past a moored compartment boat train. (BW)

One of the smaller oil tankers, *Ennerdale*, passing Castleford yard in July 1961. It could reach any of the oil wharves which, at this time, were at Leeds, Fleet, Castleford and Wakefield.

A larger oil tanker passes empty downstream through Ferrybridge Flood Lock around 1975. Note how the lock is not uniform in shape, a result of extensions over the years. The wide section by the boats stern is actually the former entrance to a basin.

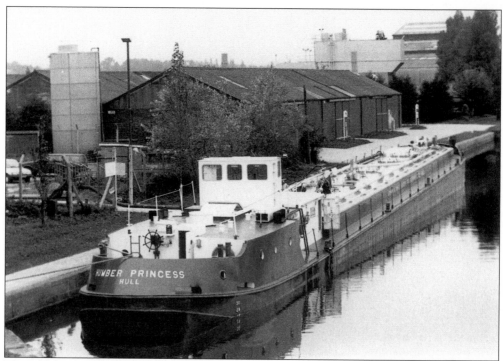

The oil wharf at Castleford about 1980, with *Humber Princess* halfway through unloading. The storage tanks are off the picture to the left. This wharf is still in use.

Winter conditions are always difficult on a waterway and none more so than when it is frozen. The winter of 1963 was one of the worst on record; here the compartment tug *Wheldale* – now preserved at the Waterways Museum at Goole – is helping general cargo boats to pass up the navigation. The jebus is being used to help as it would tend to ride up onto and thus crack the ice.

Bulk cargoes were always among the most important for the navigation. Here coal is being delivered to one of Hargreaves' wharves in Leeds around 1960. (WMG)

Ferrybridge 'A' Power Station around 1960, with many dumb boats tied up waiting to be unloaded. A train of compartments is also making its way down stream and a motor and dumb boat work upstream.

The Co-op ran a fleet of barges for household and other coal from their wharves in Leeds until the late 1970s. They had a tug, a motor boat and a number of towed dumb boats. These photos were taken in 1975, the first showing coal being loaded at Park Hill Colliery near Stanley Ferry.

Leaving Woodnook Lock on the way back to Leeds. This was the last regular traffic to use dumb boats towed on a long line. When empty, the dumb boat was kept tight up behind the motor boat on cross-straps, a system for towing which helps to steer the dumb boat. When loaded, it is necessary to keep the dumb boat away from the flow of water from the motor boat's propeller, so then they were towed on a long line.

Entering one of the locks between Castleford and Leeds. The dumb boat is being checked so that it does not stop by hitting the stern of the motor boat. Small recesses in the lock walls, many of which can still be seen, had cast iron inserts to which a hook could be fixed. A rope attached to the hook was then wound round a bollard on the boat to slow its movement.

A comparison in size, the dumb boat carrying around 90 tons of coal is passed by the *Fossdale*, an oil tanker capable of carrying 500 tons.

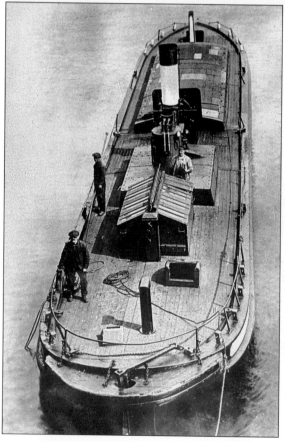

The Aire & Calder has seen dramatic changes over its three-hundred year life. The twentieth century in particular has brought about much modernization. On this page are illustrations from around 1925 when road transport was beginning to take over many traffics. The Aire & Calder's fleet of lorries, seen here outside their Dock Street offices in Leeds, were used for local deliveries, especially to Bradford where their introduction led to the closure of the Bradford Canal. The lower photograph shows one of the general cargo tugs. The hold forward of the funnel was too small to be used economically, and it was normally left empty.

In an attempt to regain traffic, British Waterways introduced their BACAT barges – Barges Aboard Catamaran – in the mid 1970s. Pushed by tugs, as in this artist's impression, they were designed to be loaded between the twin hulls of a catamaran-type ship for delivery to continental waterways. In effect they were floating containers.

One of the BACAT tugs at Goole on the occasion of the introduction of the service, 18 September 1974. The system may have reduced the work for Hull's dockers who, as a result, blacked the whole of British Waterways' fleet in the mid-1970s, despite the fact that they belonged to the same union as the British Waterways employees. The action resulted in the failure of this innovative scheme.

This must be one of the more unusual visitors to the navigation! The date is uncertain, probably between 1950 and 1960, and the location is somewhere around Wakefield. On the Aire & Calder there may even have been sufficient water for this midget submarine to submerge – but only just!

UPWARD TUGGAGE RATES

ON THE

AIRE AND CALDER NAVIGATION,

FROM AND AFTER 1st OCTOBER, 1904.

	Mean Draft or Tonnage.		Pollington.	Whitley.	Knottingley or Ferrybridge.	Bulholme Clough.	Castleford.	Fairieshill or Woodnook.	Penbank.	Foxholes.	Stanley Ferry.	Heath or Fall Ing.
			s. d.	s. d.	s. d.	s. d.	s. d.	s. d.	s. d.	s. d.	s. d.	s. d.
Vessels Drawing.	FEET.											
	5 or under ...		4 0	5 10	7 6	10 0	10 3	11 3	11 6	11 8	12 6	13 4
	5½		4 4	6 5	8 3	11 0	11 3	12 5	12 7	12 10	13 9	14 8
	6		4 9	7 0	9 0	12 0	12 3	13 6	13 9	14 0	15 0	16 0
Vessels Carrying.	TONS.											
	50 or under ...		4 0	5 10	7 6	10 0	10 3	11 3	11 6	11 8	12 6	13 4
	55		4 4	6 5	8 3	11 0	11 3	12 5	12 7	12 10	13 9	14 8
	60		4 9	7 0	9 0	12 0	12 3	13 6	13 9	14 0	15 0	16 0
	65		5 6	8 2	10 6	14 0	14 3	15 9	16 0	16 4	17 6	18 8
	70		6 4	9 4	12 0	16 0	16 4	18 0	18 4	18 8	20 0	21 4
	75		7 2	10 6	13 6	18 0	18 5	20 3	20 7	21 0	22 6	24 0
	80		7 11	11 8	15 0	20 0	20 5	22 6	22 11	23 4	25 0	26 8
	85		8 3	12 3	15 9	21 0	21 6	23 7	24 1	24 6	26 3	28 0
	90		8 9	12 10	16 6	22 0	22 6	24 9	25 3	25 8	27 6	29 4
	95		9 1	13 5	17 3	23 0	23 6	25 10	26 5	26 10	28 9	30 8
	100		9 6	14 0	18 0	24 0	24 6	27 0	27 6	28 0	30 0	32 0
	105		9 10	14 7	18 9	25 0	25 6	28 1	28 8	29 2	31 3	33 4
	110		10 3	15 2	19 6	26 0	26 6	29 3	29 9	30 4	32 6	34 8
	115		10 7	15 9	20 3	27 0	27 6	30 4	30 11	31 6	33 9	36 0
	120		11 0	16 4	21 0	28 0	28 6	31 6	32 0	32 8	35 0	37 4
	150		11 9	17 6	22 6	30 0	30 6	33 9	34 3	35 0	37 6	40 0

GOOLE to the enumerated places.

See back.

NOTE.—The Undertakers reserve to themselves the option to charge for Towing any Vessel on their **Tonnage** or **Draft**, when the Tonnage of any such Vessel shall reach or exceed **Fifty Tons.**

The Tonnage of all Vessels not having Tonnage Plates will be taken as Net Tonnage, in all other cases the Tonnage Plates will be taken.

The Draft of all Vessels will be subject to be tested with a Gauge for the purpose, and the charge for towing (when made upon the Draft) will be upon such ascertained Draft.

For shorter distances than **Ten Miles,** or for **Timber Vessels having Alongsiders,** or in cases of **Flood** or **Ice,** the Undertakers do not bind themselves to the above Rates, but reserve to themselves the right to make special ones in such cases.

377—1904.

By the 1960s, pleasure use of the waterways was developing and three ex-Leeds & Liverpool boats were converted for use as trip boats. They are seen here at Leeds waiting to take guests down to Knostrop for the opening of the new depot in June 1958.

On the same occasion, the Mayor and Mayoress of Leeds make their way through Leeds Lock on board the navigation's inspection launch, *Baranne*.

One of the trip boats, *Water Princess*, was formerly the *Wharf* of Canal Transport Limited, and is seen here passing one of the locks between Castleford and Leeds.

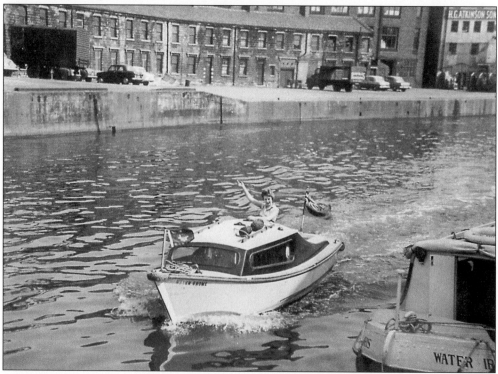

British Waterways had its own fleet of hire boats from the 1960s; an exhibition was held at Leeds to advertise them. This view of *Water Gnome* was taken outside the Dock Street offices.

The trip boats were also used for inspections. Here members of the British Waterways Board are inspecting the navigation below Knottingley. Judging from the straightness of the compartment boat train, it cannot have been very windy.

In 1981 the Inland Waterways Association held their National Rally in Leeds to draw attention to the decline in commercial carrying and to the opportunities for development along the waterfront in Leeds. Here pleasure boats crowd into Dock Street basin, formerly the preserve of commercial boats. Today boats can no longer use this arm, but the brick buildings, such as the Flyboat Warehouse seen here, have been converted for residential use. (HA)

The big change at Goole is the decline in the number of people needed to handle cargoes. These two photographs show the olden days, when everything needed to be handled individually. (WMG)

In the 1960s, there was still a considerable volume of goods passing through Goole which was carried by barge, though road transport was taking over as this photo of West Dock shows. (WMG)

It is only in the last twenty years or so that goods have tended to be put in containers or on pallets. Previously everything was loose, such as these barrels, possibly butter or bacon from Scandinavia, in the process of transshipment. The change has resulted in a drastic reduction in employment. (WMG)

Cranes have also developed, from this hydraulically powered forty-ton crane loading a road crane, to the fifty-ton electric crane now used for heavy lifts. (WMG)

Another view of West Dock with barges transshipping, now a rare sight. The tractors in the foreground are further indication of the variety of traffic handled by the port. (WMG)

Coal has ceased to be a cargo exported through the port. After the compartment boats ceased in 1986, coal continued to be delivered by rail for a short time, but this has also finished. These two photos show the final methods for loading coal. In the picture above the wagon has been lifted and tipped by the fifty-ton crane, while below is one of the coal tippers. Both were in Railway Dock and the crane is still surviving. (WMG)

Unloading timber in West Dock from the Russian boat MV *Oterya* in 1969. This was the first cargo of timber from Joensuu, Finland, to come direct through the Saimaa Canal which links the Finnish lakes to the Baltic via Russia. (WMG)

Loading machinery for Finland by crane in Railway Dock in the 1960s. (WMG)

Eight

The Navigation Today

A barge carrying sand at Goole on its way up the navigation in the spring of 1999. In the background can be seen the navigation's former workshop site and the 1960s buildings used for repairing compartment boats. Warehousing and wharf facilities have now been erected here to form Associated British Ports new Caldaire Terminal. On the left is the preserved No.5 Compartment Boat Hoist, access to which can be arranged through the Waterways Museum at Goole.

Coal is still brought to Ferrybridge Power Station in pans. The building in the centre houses the unloading apparatus which lifts each pan out of the water and then tips it to unload the coal much in the same way as the earlier compartment boat system.

With greater awareness of the environmental benefits of water transport, traffic is coming back to the navigation. This recent photo shows Whittakers' Humber Energy leaving Fleet Oil Storage Depot after unloading the first waterborne cargo of oil to arrive here for a number of years. (BW)

South Dock, Goole, with one of Whittakers' tankers making its way back to the Humber. In the background is the preserved No.5 compartment boat hoist. The *Sola* is a typical river-sea vessel: increasing numbers of this kind of vessel are visiting the port. Registered on Poland's Baltic coast, she brings regular cargoes of grain to the port.

Goole Docks pictured recently from the top of the new water tower. Note how general cargoes are now palletised or containerised, making their handling much simpler and more efficient.

Although compartments are no longer repaired at Stanley Ferry, the repair shed is still busy producing lock gates for many of British Waterways' canals. This photo was taken during an open day in the early 1990s, and shows a pair of wooden lock gates destined for the Calder & Hebble.

Thwaite Mill was one of the mills which caused the navigation so many problems in the eighteenth century. It was subsequently purchased by the navigation and was used for many years for making putty. Raw materials were brought by the navigation and unloaded by the wharf crane which can just be seen behind the house on the right. Today the mill, complete with water wheels and machinery, is open to the public as a museum.

The Armouries Museum. The boatmen who used Clarence Dock in its heyday would certainly have difficulty recognizing it today.

The former warehouses at Leeds, Dock Street, have now been converted to residential use. New uses are keeping many old waterside buildings alive, though it is a pity that the old arm is no longer available for boats.

During the First World War, several Aire & Calder tugs were sent to France to help on French waterways. More recently, the *Pauline*, one of three surviving Aire & Calder flyboats, also made the trip, spending eighteen months travelling across France, Belgium and the Netherlands.

The old river bed at St Aidans revealed some real archaeological finds after it was drained following problems with the adjacent opencast coal workings. The remains of several clinker-built keels were found, some possibly two hundred years old. Only one other site with such boat remains is known, so it was important that these remains were recorded, a task which has now almost been completed. Here a group of volunteers inspect the stern post of one of the boats.

The best place to find out more about the history of the Aire & Calder is the Waterways Museum at Goole, winner of the Museum of the Year Award in 1996. The museum is part of the Sobriety Project, an educational charity formed in 1973 which uses the history, environment and arts of the Yorkshire waterways as a resource for learning and regeneration. The organisation takes its name from the Humber keel *Sobriety*, seen here passing through Sykehouse Lock on the New Junction Canal. The museum also has an extensive archive, and a café and shop complement the museum attractions.

Other attractions include the tug *Wheldale* and several 'Tom Puddings', along with former grain barge *Room 58*, now a small art gallery and conference centre. A nature trail has been developed alongside the canal, including an iron-age board walk, reed beds and willow plantations which provide the raw materials for coracle-building and art work.

The Sobriety Project's sailing barge *Audrey* began life in 1915 as a light ship on the Humber. Acquired in 1987, she has been converted to a gaff rigged ketch, similar to many Goole 'billyboys'. She has cruised widely, taking community and other groups around the British and European coast. Here she is seen sailing on the Humber with the sloop *Amy Howson* and the keel *Comrade*.

Acknowledgements

Many thanks to the following people and organizations for permission to use their photographs:

Harry Arnold (HA)
Stanley Brown (p.36, bottom)
Paul and Gabrielle Lorenz (p.124)
Roy Parker (p.120, bottom)
Associated British Ports (ABP)
British Waterways (BW)
The Fowler Collection, Rural History Centre,
    University of Reading (p.23, bottom)
Leeds City Library (LCL)
Wakefield Metropolitan District Council,
    Libraries and Information Service (WMDC)
The Waterways Museum at Goole (WMG)
The *Yorkshire Post* (p.104, bottom)